50 Italian Ice Cream Recipes for Home

By: Kelly Johnson

Table of Contents

- Classic Vanilla Gelato
- Pistachio Gelato
- Stracciatella Gelato
- Hazelnut Gelato
- Tiramisu Gelato
- Chocolate Hazelnut Gelato
- Lemon Sorbetto
- Mango Sorbetto
- Coffee Gelato
- Ricotta and Fig Gelato
- Limoncello Sorbetto
- Dark Chocolate Gelato
- Vanilla Bean Gelato
- Almond Gelato
- Cherry Gelato
- Salted Caramel Gelato
- Strawberry Gelato
- Peach Gelato
- Mixed Berry Sorbetto
- Italian Coffee Sorbetto
- Fennel and Honey Gelato
- Pineapple Sorbetto
- Grapefruit Sorbetto
- Mascarpone Gelato with Blueberries
- Cinnamon Gelato
- Chocolate Gelato with Cherries
- Chestnut Gelato
- Cantaloupe Sorbetto
- Coconut Gelato
- Vanilla and Cardamom Gelato
- Raspberry Sorbetto
- Apricot Gelato
- Mixed Nut Gelato
- Walnut Gelato
- Saffron Gelato

- Apple Gelato with Cinnamon
- Italian Ricotta Ice Cream
- Ricotta and Chocolate Chip Gelato
- Olive Oil Gelato
- Amaretto Gelato
- Pear Sorbetto
- Poppy Seed Gelato
- Vanilla and Lavender Gelato
- Banana and Honey Gelato
- Pistachio and Strawberry Gelato
- Italian Fruit Salad Sorbetto
- Pomegranate Sorbetto
- Spiced Pear Gelato
- Limoncello and Mint Gelato
- Ricotta and Orange Gelato

Classic Vanilla Gelato

Ingredients:

- 2 cups whole milk
- 1 cup heavy cream
- 3/4 cup sugar
- 1 vanilla bean, split and scraped (or 2 tsp vanilla extract)
- 4 egg yolks

Instructions:

1. In a saucepan, combine the milk, cream, and vanilla bean. Heat until just below boiling, then remove from heat.
2. In a bowl, whisk together the egg yolks and sugar until smooth.
3. Gradually pour the warm milk mixture into the egg yolks, whisking constantly to temper the eggs.
4. Return the mixture to the saucepan and cook over low heat, stirring constantly until it thickens.
5. Strain the mixture and let it cool completely. Once cooled, chill in the refrigerator for at least 2 hours.
6. Pour into an ice cream maker and churn according to the manufacturer's instructions.
7. Freeze for at least 4 hours before serving.

Pistachio Gelato

Ingredients:

- 2 cups whole milk
- 1 cup heavy cream
- 3/4 cup sugar
- 3/4 cup shelled pistachios
- 4 egg yolks
- 1 tsp vanilla extract

Instructions:

1. In a saucepan, combine the milk, cream, and pistachios. Heat until just below boiling, then remove from heat.
2. Let the pistachios steep in the mixture for 10 minutes, then blend the mixture to a smooth consistency.
3. In a separate bowl, whisk the egg yolks and sugar until pale and smooth.
4. Gradually add the pistachio mixture into the egg yolks, whisking constantly. Return to the pan and cook over low heat until thickened.
5. Strain the mixture and chill for 2 hours. Once chilled, churn in an ice cream maker according to manufacturer's instructions.

Stracciatella Gelato

Ingredients:

- 2 cups whole milk
- 1 cup heavy cream
- 3/4 cup sugar
- 4 egg yolks
- 1/2 cup dark chocolate, finely chopped

Instructions:

1. Prepare the base by heating milk, cream, and sugar in a saucepan. Stir until the sugar dissolves.
2. In a separate bowl, whisk the egg yolks and then gradually add the warm milk mixture, whisking constantly.
3. Pour the mixture back into the saucepan and cook over low heat, stirring until it thickens.
4. Once thickened, remove from heat, strain, and let it cool.
5. Pour the mixture into an ice cream maker and churn.
6. In the final minutes of churning, add the finely chopped chocolate to form delicate chocolate shards.

Hazelnut Gelato

Ingredients:

- 2 cups whole milk
- 1 cup heavy cream
- 3/4 cup sugar
- 1/2 cup roasted hazelnuts
- 4 egg yolks
- 1 tsp vanilla extract

Instructions:

1. Heat the milk, cream, and roasted hazelnuts together in a saucepan until just below boiling. Remove from heat and let the hazelnuts steep for 10 minutes.
2. Blend the mixture until smooth, then strain out the hazelnuts.
3. Whisk together the egg yolks and sugar. Gradually add the warm milk mixture to the yolks.
4. Return to the stove and cook until the mixture thickens. Strain and chill for 2 hours.
5. Churn the mixture in an ice cream maker according to manufacturer's instructions.

Tiramisu Gelato

Ingredients:

- 2 cups whole milk
- 1 cup heavy cream
- 3/4 cup sugar
- 4 egg yolks
- 2 tbsp mascarpone cheese
- 1/4 cup strong brewed coffee
- 1 tbsp coffee liqueur (optional)
- Cocoa powder for garnish

Instructions:

1. In a saucepan, combine the milk, cream, and sugar. Heat until just below boiling.
2. In a bowl, whisk the egg yolks, then gradually add the milk mixture while whisking constantly.
3. Cook the mixture over low heat until thickened, then remove from heat.
4. Stir in the mascarpone cheese, coffee, and coffee liqueur (if using).
5. Let the mixture cool, then churn in an ice cream maker according to the manufacturer's instructions.
6. Garnish with a dusting of cocoa powder before serving.

Chocolate Hazelnut Gelato

Ingredients:

- 2 cups whole milk
- 1 cup heavy cream
- 3/4 cup sugar
- 1/2 cup hazelnut paste
- 1/2 cup cocoa powder
- 4 egg yolks

Instructions:

1. Heat the milk, cream, and sugar together in a saucepan. Add the hazelnut paste and cocoa powder, stirring until smooth.
2. Whisk the egg yolks and add the warm milk mixture gradually.
3. Cook the mixture over low heat until thickened, then strain and cool.
4. Churn in an ice cream maker according to manufacturer's instructions.

Lemon Sorbetto

Ingredients:

- 2 cups water
- 1 cup sugar
- 1 cup fresh lemon juice
- Zest of 1 lemon

Instructions:

1. In a saucepan, combine the water and sugar. Heat over medium heat until the sugar dissolves.
2. Let the syrup cool, then stir in the lemon juice and zest.
3. Freeze the mixture in an ice cream maker according to the manufacturer's instructions.
4. Transfer to a container and freeze for at least 4 hours before serving.

Mango Sorbetto

Ingredients:

- 3 cups fresh mango puree
- 1 cup water
- 3/4 cup sugar
- 1 tbsp lime juice

Instructions:

1. Combine the mango puree, water, sugar, and lime juice in a bowl.
2. Stir until the sugar dissolves and freeze in an ice cream maker according to the manufacturer's instructions.
3. Transfer to a container and freeze for at least 4 hours before serving.

Coffee Gelato

Ingredients:

- 2 cups whole milk
- 1 cup heavy cream
- 3/4 cup sugar
- 4 egg yolks
- 1/4 cup strong brewed coffee
- 1 tsp vanilla extract

Instructions:

1. Heat the milk, cream, and sugar together in a saucepan.
2. In a bowl, whisk the egg yolks, then gradually add the warm milk mixture.
3. Cook over low heat until thickened, then strain and stir in the coffee and vanilla extract.
4. Chill for 2 hours, then churn in an ice cream maker according to the manufacturer's instructions.

Ricotta and Fig Gelato

Ingredients:

- 2 cups whole milk
- 1 cup heavy cream
- 3/4 cup sugar
- 1 cup ricotta cheese
- 1/2 cup dried figs, chopped
- 4 egg yolks
- 1 tsp vanilla extract

Instructions:

1. In a saucepan, heat the milk and cream together. Add the chopped figs and cook until softened. Remove from heat and let cool.
2. Blend the ricotta cheese and milk-fig mixture until smooth.
3. In a bowl, whisk the egg yolks and sugar until pale.
4. Gradually add the warm ricotta mixture into the yolks, stirring constantly.
5. Return the mixture to the saucepan and cook over low heat until thickened. Strain and let cool.
6. Once cooled, chill in the fridge for 2 hours. Churn in an ice cream maker according to manufacturer's instructions.

Limoncello Sorbetto

Ingredients:

- 2 cups water
- 1 cup sugar
- 1 cup fresh lemon juice
- 1/4 cup limoncello liqueur
- Zest of 2 lemons

Instructions:

1. In a saucepan, combine water and sugar. Heat over medium heat, stirring until the sugar dissolves.
2. Remove from heat and stir in lemon juice, limoncello, and zest. Let the mixture cool.
3. Pour into an ice cream maker and churn according to the manufacturer's instructions.
4. Transfer to a container and freeze for at least 4 hours before serving.

Dark Chocolate Gelato

Ingredients:

- 2 cups whole milk
- 1 cup heavy cream
- 3/4 cup sugar
- 1/2 cup dark chocolate (70% cocoa), chopped
- 4 egg yolks
- 1 tsp vanilla extract

Instructions:

1. Heat the milk and cream together in a saucepan. Once heated, add the chopped dark chocolate and stir until melted and smooth.
2. In a bowl, whisk together the egg yolks and sugar.
3. Gradually add the chocolate mixture into the egg yolks, stirring constantly.
4. Return the mixture to the saucepan and cook over low heat until thickened. Strain and let cool.
5. Chill the mixture in the refrigerator for 2 hours, then churn in an ice cream maker.

Vanilla Bean Gelato

Ingredients:

- 2 cups whole milk
- 1 cup heavy cream
- 3/4 cup sugar
- 4 egg yolks
- 1 vanilla bean, split and scraped (or 2 tsp vanilla extract)

Instructions:

1. Heat the milk and cream in a saucepan with the vanilla bean. Bring to a simmer and remove from heat.
2. In a separate bowl, whisk the egg yolks and sugar until pale and smooth.
3. Gradually add the warm milk mixture into the egg yolks, whisking constantly.
4. Return the mixture to the saucepan and cook over low heat until thickened.
5. Strain and chill the mixture in the refrigerator for 2 hours. Churn in an ice cream maker according to the manufacturer's instructions.

Almond Gelato

Ingredients:

- 2 cups whole milk
- 1 cup heavy cream
- 3/4 cup sugar
- 1/2 cup almond paste or almond meal
- 4 egg yolks
- 1 tsp vanilla extract

Instructions:

1. Heat the milk and cream together in a saucepan. Add the almond paste or almond meal and whisk until smooth.
2. In a separate bowl, whisk the egg yolks and sugar until pale.
3. Gradually add the warm almond mixture into the egg yolks, stirring constantly.
4. Return the mixture to the saucepan and cook over low heat until thickened. Strain and let cool.
5. Chill for 2 hours and churn in an ice cream maker according to the manufacturer's instructions.

Cherry Gelato

Ingredients:

- 2 cups whole milk
- 1 cup heavy cream
- 3/4 cup sugar
- 1 cup fresh or frozen cherries, pitted
- 4 egg yolks
- 1 tsp vanilla extract

Instructions:

1. In a saucepan, heat the milk and cream together. Add the cherries and cook until soft.
2. Blend the cherry mixture until smooth and strain to remove the solids.
3. In a bowl, whisk the egg yolks and sugar until pale.
4. Gradually add the cherry mixture into the yolks, whisking constantly.
5. Return the mixture to the saucepan and cook over low heat until thickened. Strain and cool.
6. Chill in the fridge for 2 hours, then churn in an ice cream maker.

Salted Caramel Gelato

Ingredients:

- 2 cups whole milk
- 1 cup heavy cream
- 3/4 cup sugar
- 1/2 cup caramel sauce (store-bought or homemade)
- 1/4 tsp sea salt
- 4 egg yolks

Instructions:

1. In a saucepan, heat the milk and cream together. Stir in the caramel sauce and sea salt until smooth.
2. In a bowl, whisk the egg yolks and sugar until smooth.
3. Gradually add the warm caramel mixture into the yolks, whisking constantly.
4. Return to the saucepan and cook over low heat until thickened. Strain and cool.
5. Chill for 2 hours, then churn in an ice cream maker.

Strawberry Gelato

Ingredients:

- 2 cups whole milk
- 1 cup heavy cream
- 3/4 cup sugar
- 1 1/2 cups fresh strawberries, hulled and pureed
- 4 egg yolks

Instructions:

1. Heat the milk and cream in a saucepan until warm.
2. In a bowl, whisk the egg yolks and sugar until pale and smooth.
3. Gradually add the warm milk mixture into the egg yolks, whisking constantly.
4. Return the mixture to the saucepan and cook over low heat until thickened. Strain and cool.
5. Add the strawberry puree, mix well, and chill for 2 hours.
6. Churn in an ice cream maker according to the manufacturer's instructions.

Peach Gelato

Ingredients:

- 2 cups whole milk
- 1 cup heavy cream
- 3/4 cup sugar
- 2 ripe peaches, peeled and pureed
- 4 egg yolks
- 1 tsp vanilla extract

Instructions:

1. Heat the milk and cream in a saucepan. In a separate bowl, whisk the egg yolks and sugar.
2. Gradually add the warm milk mixture into the yolks, whisking constantly.
3. Return the mixture to the saucepan and cook over low heat until thickened. Strain and cool.
4. Once cooled, stir in the peach puree and vanilla extract.
5. Chill for 2 hours and churn in an ice cream maker.

Mixed Berry Sorbetto

Ingredients:

- 2 cups mixed berries (strawberries, raspberries, blueberries)
- 1 cup water
- 3/4 cup sugar
- 1 tbsp lemon juice

Instructions:

1. In a saucepan, combine water and sugar. Heat over medium heat until the sugar dissolves.
2. Add the berries and cook until softened. Blend until smooth.
3. Stir in the lemon juice and let the mixture cool.
4. Pour into an ice cream maker and churn according to the manufacturer's instructions.
5. Freeze for at least 4 hours before serving.

Italian Coffee Sorbetto

Ingredients:

- 2 cups water
- 1 cup sugar
- 1/2 cup strong brewed espresso or coffee
- 1 tbsp vanilla extract

Instructions:

1. In a saucepan, combine water and sugar, and heat until the sugar dissolves.
2. Add the brewed coffee and vanilla extract, stirring to combine.
3. Let the mixture cool completely.
4. Pour into an ice cream maker and churn according to the manufacturer's instructions.
5. Freeze for at least 4 hours before serving.

Fennel and Honey Gelato

Ingredients:

- 2 cups whole milk
- 1 cup heavy cream
- 3/4 cup sugar
- 1 bulb fennel, finely chopped
- 3 tbsp honey
- 4 egg yolks
- 1 tsp vanilla extract

Instructions:

1. In a saucepan, heat the milk and cream. Add the fennel and simmer for 10 minutes.
2. Strain out the fennel and return the milk-cream mixture to the pot.
3. In a bowl, whisk the egg yolks and sugar until smooth.
4. Gradually add the warm milk mixture into the yolks, stirring constantly.
5. Cook over low heat until thickened. Strain and let cool.
6. Stir in honey and vanilla, chill the mixture for 2 hours, and churn in an ice cream maker.

Pineapple Sorbetto

Ingredients:

- 2 cups fresh pineapple, chopped
- 1 cup water
- 3/4 cup sugar
- 1 tbsp lemon juice

Instructions:

1. In a blender, combine the pineapple, water, sugar, and lemon juice. Blend until smooth.
2. Strain the mixture to remove any solids.
3. Pour into an ice cream maker and churn according to the manufacturer's instructions.
4. Freeze for at least 4 hours before serving.

Grapefruit Sorbetto

Ingredients:

- 2 cups fresh grapefruit juice
- 1 cup water
- 3/4 cup sugar
- Zest of 1 grapefruit

Instructions:

1. In a saucepan, heat water and sugar until the sugar dissolves.
2. Stir in the grapefruit juice and zest.
3. Let the mixture cool to room temperature, then chill in the fridge for 2 hours.
4. Pour into an ice cream maker and churn according to the manufacturer's instructions.
5. Freeze for at least 4 hours before serving.

Mascarpone Gelato with Blueberries

Ingredients:

- 1 1/2 cups mascarpone cheese
- 2 cups whole milk
- 1 cup heavy cream
- 3/4 cup sugar
- 1 cup fresh blueberries
- 4 egg yolks

Instructions:

1. In a saucepan, heat the milk and cream until just warm.
2. In a bowl, whisk the egg yolks and sugar until smooth.
3. Gradually add the warm milk mixture into the egg yolks, stirring constantly.
4. Return to the saucepan and cook over low heat until thickened.
5. Strain and let the mixture cool. Stir in mascarpone cheese and blueberry puree.
6. Chill for 2 hours, then churn in an ice cream maker.

Cinnamon Gelato

Ingredients:

- 2 cups whole milk
- 1 cup heavy cream
- 3/4 cup sugar
- 1 tbsp cinnamon
- 4 egg yolks

Instructions:

1. In a saucepan, heat the milk and cream with cinnamon until warm.
2. In a separate bowl, whisk the egg yolks and sugar until smooth.
3. Gradually add the warm milk mixture into the yolks, whisking constantly.
4. Return to the saucepan and cook over low heat until thickened.
5. Strain and let cool.
6. Chill for 2 hours and churn in an ice cream maker.

Chocolate Gelato with Cherries

Ingredients:

- 2 cups whole milk
- 1 cup heavy cream
- 1/2 cup sugar
- 4 oz dark chocolate (70% cocoa), chopped
- 1 cup fresh cherries, pitted and chopped
- 4 egg yolks
- 1 tsp vanilla extract

Instructions:

1. In a saucepan, heat the milk and cream together. Add the dark chocolate and stir until smooth.
2. In a bowl, whisk the egg yolks and sugar until pale and smooth.
3. Gradually add the warm chocolate mixture into the yolks, stirring constantly.
4. Return to the saucepan and cook over low heat until thickened.
5. Strain and let cool. Once cooled, stir in the chopped cherries.
6. Chill for 2 hours, then churn in an ice cream maker.

Chestnut Gelato

Ingredients:

- 2 cups whole milk
- 1 cup heavy cream
- 3/4 cup sugar
- 1 cup chestnut puree
- 4 egg yolks

Instructions:

1. In a saucepan, heat the milk and cream together.
2. In a separate bowl, whisk the egg yolks and sugar until smooth.
3. Gradually add the warm milk mixture into the yolks, whisking constantly.
4. Return to the saucepan and cook over low heat until thickened.
5. Stir in the chestnut puree and strain the mixture.
6. Let it cool, then chill in the refrigerator for 2 hours. Churn in an ice cream maker.

Cantaloupe Sorbetto

Ingredients:

- 2 cups fresh cantaloupe, chopped
- 1 cup water
- 3/4 cup sugar
- 1 tbsp lemon juice

Instructions:

1. Blend the cantaloupe, water, sugar, and lemon juice until smooth.
2. Strain the mixture to remove any solids.
3. Pour into an ice cream maker and churn according to the manufacturer's instructions.
4. Freeze for at least 4 hours before serving.

Coconut Gelato

Ingredients:

- 2 cups whole milk
- 1 cup coconut cream
- 3/4 cup sugar
- 4 egg yolks
- 1 tsp vanilla extract

Instructions:

1. In a saucepan, heat the milk and coconut cream together.
2. In a bowl, whisk the egg yolks and sugar until smooth.
3. Gradually add the warm milk mixture into the yolks, stirring constantly.
4. Return to the saucepan and cook over low heat until thickened.
5. Strain and let cool.
6. Chill for 2 hours, then churn in an ice cream maker.

Vanilla and Cardamom Gelato

Ingredients:

- 2 cups whole milk
- 1 cup heavy cream
- 3/4 cup sugar
- 1 vanilla bean (or 2 tsp vanilla extract)
- 1 tsp ground cardamom
- 4 egg yolks

Instructions:

1. In a saucepan, heat the milk and cream together. If using a vanilla bean, split and scrape the seeds into the milk mixture. Simmer for 10 minutes, then strain to remove the bean.
2. Whisk the egg yolks and sugar until smooth.
3. Gradually add the warm milk mixture into the yolks, stirring constantly.
4. Return to the saucepan and cook over low heat until thickened.
5. Strain and let cool. Stir in the ground cardamom.
6. Chill the mixture for 2 hours, then churn in an ice cream maker.

Raspberry Sorbetto

Ingredients:

- 2 cups fresh raspberries
- 1 cup water
- 3/4 cup sugar
- 1 tbsp lemon juice

Instructions:

1. Blend the raspberries with water, sugar, and lemon juice until smooth.
2. Strain the mixture to remove the seeds.
3. Pour into an ice cream maker and churn according to the manufacturer's instructions.
4. Freeze for at least 4 hours before serving.

Apricot Gelato

Ingredients:

- 2 cups fresh apricots, peeled and chopped
- 1 cup whole milk
- 1 cup heavy cream
- 3/4 cup sugar
- 4 egg yolks
- 1 tsp lemon juice

Instructions:

1. In a saucepan, combine the milk and cream. Heat until warm.
2. In a blender, blend the apricots with the lemon juice until smooth.
3. Whisk the egg yolks and sugar until smooth.
4. Gradually add the warm milk mixture into the yolks, stirring constantly.
5. Return to the saucepan and cook over low heat until thickened.
6. Strain the mixture and let it cool.
7. Chill for 2 hours, then churn in an ice cream maker. Stir in the apricot puree before churning.

Mixed Nut Gelato

Ingredients:

- 2 cups whole milk
- 1 cup heavy cream
- 3/4 cup sugar
- 1/2 cup mixed nuts (hazelnuts, almonds, pistachios, etc.), chopped
- 4 egg yolks
- 1 tsp vanilla extract

Instructions:

1. In a saucepan, heat the milk and cream.
2. In a separate bowl, whisk the egg yolks and sugar until smooth.
3. Gradually add the warm milk mixture into the yolks, stirring constantly.
4. Return to the saucepan and cook over low heat until thickened.
5. Stir in the chopped nuts and vanilla extract.
6. Strain and let it cool. Chill for 2 hours, then churn in an ice cream maker.

Walnut Gelato

Ingredients:

- 2 cups whole milk
- 1 cup heavy cream
- 3/4 cup sugar
- 1 cup walnuts, toasted and chopped
- 4 egg yolks
- 1 tsp vanilla extract

Instructions:

1. In a saucepan, heat the milk and cream together.
2. Whisk the egg yolks and sugar until smooth.
3. Gradually add the warm milk mixture into the yolks, stirring constantly.
4. Return to the saucepan and cook over low heat until thickened.
5. Strain and let it cool.
6. Toast and chop the walnuts, then stir them into the gelato mixture before churning.
7. Chill for 2 hours, then churn in an ice cream maker.

Saffron Gelato

Ingredients:

- 2 cups whole milk
- 1 cup heavy cream
- 3/4 cup sugar
- 1/2 tsp saffron threads
- 4 egg yolks
- 1 tsp vanilla extract

Instructions:

1. In a saucepan, heat the milk and cream until warm.
2. Add the saffron threads to the milk mixture and steep for 10 minutes.
3. Whisk the egg yolks and sugar until smooth.
4. Gradually add the warm milk mixture into the yolks, stirring constantly.
5. Return to the saucepan and cook over low heat until thickened.
6. Strain and let it cool.
7. Chill for 2 hours, then churn in an ice cream maker.

Apple Gelato with Cinnamon

Ingredients:

- 2 cups whole milk
- 1 cup heavy cream
- 3/4 cup sugar
- 2 apples, peeled, cored, and chopped
- 1 tsp cinnamon
- 4 egg yolks

Instructions:

1. In a saucepan, heat the milk and cream.
2. In a blender, puree the apples with cinnamon until smooth.
3. Whisk the egg yolks and sugar until smooth.
4. Gradually add the warm milk mixture into the yolks, stirring constantly.
5. Return to the saucepan and cook over low heat until thickened.
6. Strain the mixture and let it cool.
7. Chill for 2 hours, then churn in an ice cream maker. Stir in the apple puree before churning.

Italian Ricotta Ice Cream

Ingredients:

- 2 cups ricotta cheese
- 1 cup heavy cream
- 3/4 cup sugar
- 1 tsp vanilla extract
- Zest of 1 lemon

Instructions:

1. In a bowl, combine the ricotta cheese, cream, sugar, vanilla, and lemon zest.
2. Blend until smooth and creamy.
3. Chill the mixture for 2 hours.
4. Pour into an ice cream maker and churn according to the manufacturer's instructions.

Ricotta and Chocolate Chip Gelato

Ingredients:

- 2 cups ricotta cheese
- 1 cup heavy cream
- 3/4 cup sugar
- 1/2 cup mini chocolate chips
- 1 tsp vanilla extract
- Zest of 1 lemon

Instructions:

1. In a bowl, combine the ricotta, cream, sugar, vanilla, and lemon zest. Blend until smooth.
2. Stir in the chocolate chips.
3. Chill for 2 hours, then churn in an ice cream maker.

Olive Oil Gelato

Ingredients:

- 2 cups whole milk
- 1 cup heavy cream
- 1/2 cup extra virgin olive oil
- 3/4 cup sugar
- 4 egg yolks
- 1 tsp vanilla extract

Instructions:

1. In a saucepan, heat the milk and cream together.
2. In a bowl, whisk the egg yolks and sugar until smooth.
3. Gradually add the warm milk mixture into the yolks, stirring constantly.
4. Return to the saucepan and cook over low heat until thickened.
5. Stir in the olive oil and vanilla extract.
6. Strain and let it cool. Chill for 2 hours, then churn in an ice cream maker.

Amaretto Gelato

Ingredients:

- 2 cups whole milk
- 1 cup heavy cream
- 3/4 cup sugar
- 1/4 cup Amaretto liqueur
- 4 egg yolks
- 1 tsp vanilla extract

Instructions:

1. In a saucepan, heat the milk and cream until warm.
2. In a bowl, whisk the egg yolks and sugar until smooth.
3. Gradually add the warm milk mixture into the yolks, stirring constantly.
4. Return to the saucepan and cook over low heat until thickened.
5. Stir in the Amaretto liqueur and vanilla extract.
6. Strain and let it cool.
7. Chill for 2 hours, then churn in an ice cream maker.

Pear Sorbetto

Ingredients:

- 4 ripe pears, peeled and chopped
- 1 cup water
- 1/2 cup sugar
- 1 tbsp lemon juice

Instructions:

1. Blend the pears with water, sugar, and lemon juice until smooth.
2. Strain the mixture to remove any solids.
3. Pour into an ice cream maker and churn according to the manufacturer's instructions.
4. Freeze for at least 4 hours before serving.

Poppy Seed Gelato

Ingredients:

- 2 cups whole milk
- 1 cup heavy cream
- 3/4 cup sugar
- 2 tbsp poppy seeds
- 4 egg yolks
- 1 tsp vanilla extract

Instructions:

1. In a saucepan, heat the milk and cream together.
2. Whisk the egg yolks and sugar until smooth.
3. Gradually add the warm milk mixture into the yolks, stirring constantly.
4. Return to the saucepan and cook over low heat until thickened.
5. Stir in the poppy seeds and vanilla extract.
6. Strain and let it cool.
7. Chill for 2 hours, then churn in an ice cream maker.

Vanilla and Lavender Gelato

Ingredients:

- 2 cups whole milk
- 1 cup heavy cream
- 3/4 cup sugar
- 1 tbsp dried lavender flowers
- 1 vanilla bean (or 1 tsp vanilla extract)
- 4 egg yolks

Instructions:

1. In a saucepan, heat the milk and cream with the lavender and vanilla bean (or extract). Let it steep for about 10 minutes, then strain.
2. Whisk the egg yolks and sugar until smooth.
3. Gradually add the warm milk mixture into the yolks, stirring constantly.
4. Return to the saucepan and cook over low heat until thickened.
5. Strain again and let it cool.
6. Chill for 2 hours, then churn in an ice cream maker.

Banana and Honey Gelato

Ingredients:

- 2 ripe bananas, mashed
- 2 cups whole milk
- 1 cup heavy cream
- 1/2 cup honey
- 4 egg yolks
- 1 tsp vanilla extract

Instructions:

1. In a saucepan, heat the milk and cream together.
2. Whisk the egg yolks and honey until smooth.
3. Gradually add the warm milk mixture into the yolks, stirring constantly.
4. Return to the saucepan and cook over low heat until thickened.
5. Stir in the mashed bananas and vanilla extract.
6. Strain and let it cool.
7. Chill for 2 hours, then churn in an ice cream maker.

Pistachio and Strawberry Gelato

Ingredients:

- 1 cup pistachios, shelled and chopped
- 2 cups whole milk
- 1 cup heavy cream
- 3/4 cup sugar
- 4 egg yolks
- 1 cup fresh strawberries, puréed
- 1 tsp vanilla extract

Instructions:

1. In a saucepan, heat the milk and cream together.
2. Whisk the egg yolks and sugar until smooth.
3. Gradually add the warm milk mixture into the yolks, stirring constantly.
4. Return to the saucepan and cook over low heat until thickened.
5. Stir in the pistachios, strawberry purée, and vanilla extract.
6. Strain and let it cool.
7. Chill for 2 hours, then churn in an ice cream maker.

Italian Fruit Salad Sorbetto

Ingredients:

- 1 cup diced watermelon
- 1 cup diced cantaloupe
- 1 cup diced honeydew melon
- 1/2 cup fresh orange juice
- 1/4 cup sugar
- 1 tbsp lemon juice

Instructions:

1. Blend the watermelon, cantaloupe, and honeydew melon together until smooth.
2. Add the orange juice, sugar, and lemon juice, and blend until combined.
3. Strain the mixture to remove any solids.
4. Pour into an ice cream maker and churn according to the manufacturer's instructions.
5. Freeze for at least 4 hours before serving.

Pomegranate Sorbetto

Ingredients:

- 2 cups pomegranate juice
- 1/2 cup sugar
- 1 tbsp lemon juice

Instructions:

1. Combine the pomegranate juice, sugar, and lemon juice in a saucepan.
2. Heat over low heat, stirring until the sugar dissolves.
3. Let the mixture cool to room temperature.
4. Pour into an ice cream maker and churn according to the manufacturer's instructions.
5. Freeze for at least 4 hours before serving.

Spiced Pear Gelato

Ingredients:

- 2 ripe pears, peeled and chopped
- 1 cup whole milk
- 1 cup heavy cream
- 3/4 cup sugar
- 1/2 tsp cinnamon
- 1/4 tsp ground ginger
- 1/4 tsp ground nutmeg
- 4 egg yolks

Instructions:

1. In a saucepan, heat the milk and cream together with the cinnamon, ginger, and nutmeg.
2. Blend the pears until smooth, then set aside.
3. Whisk the egg yolks and sugar until smooth.
4. Gradually add the warm milk mixture into the yolks, stirring constantly.
5. Return to the saucepan and cook over low heat until thickened.
6. Stir in the pear purée and let it cool.
7. Strain and chill for 2 hours, then churn in an ice cream maker.

Limoncello and Mint Gelato

Ingredients:

- 2 cups whole milk
- 1 cup heavy cream
- 3/4 cup sugar
- 1/2 cup Limoncello liqueur
- 1/4 cup fresh mint leaves, chopped
- 4 egg yolks
- Zest of 1 lemon

Instructions:

1. In a saucepan, heat the milk and cream together.
2. Whisk the egg yolks and sugar until smooth.
3. Gradually add the warm milk mixture into the yolks, stirring constantly.
4. Return to the saucepan and cook over low heat until thickened.
5. Stir in the Limoncello, fresh mint, and lemon zest.
6. Strain and let it cool.
7. Chill for 2 hours, then churn in an ice cream maker.

Ricotta and Orange Gelato

Ingredients:

- 2 cups whole milk
- 1 cup heavy cream
- 1/2 cup ricotta cheese
- 3/4 cup sugar
- Zest of 1 orange
- 1/4 cup fresh orange juice
- 4 egg yolks

Instructions:

1. In a saucepan, heat the milk and cream together.
2. Whisk the egg yolks and sugar until smooth.
3. Gradually add the warm milk mixture into the yolks, stirring constantly.
4. Return to the saucepan and cook over low heat until thickened.
5. Stir in the ricotta cheese, orange zest, and orange juice.
6. Strain and let it cool.
7. Chill for 2 hours, then churn in an ice cream maker.

www.ingramcontent.com/pod-product-compliance
Lightning Source LLC
LaVergne TN
LVHW061955070526
838199LV00060B/4130